Her Name is Grace

POETRY ABOUT A LIFE
REDEEMED FROM HELL ON EARTH

PATRICIA ANN JOHNSON

Speak Fire
Publishing

Table of Contents

Dedication

This book is dedicated to my glorious, wonderful God. It is because of his unyielding grace and favor that I was allowed to have a voice and although the world quieted me to a whisper, God transformed the whispers of a little girl into the roar of a lion.

It is God's amazing love that changed a life filled with bitterness and suffering to a life of hope and joy that has become my purpose. That passion is the reason for my existence, my commitment to God, and earnest desire to lead women to the knowledge of whose they are and who they are through him.

I am undeserving of God's infinite love, but He allowed me His grace. This unmerited favor. This splendid love that I will never fully comprehend Why does he love me like this? Because I am HIS child! My Holy Father brought a man into my life that exposed me to the love of Jesus. A man whose heart posture was toward heaven.

Thank you, Father, for Cliffton, and the desire that he had to plant the seed of the gospel. The revelation that he helped me to attain through your word will never go back to you void.

Cliffton, thank you.

Verily your wife,
Patricia

Introduction

To my wife: As written by Cliffton

The question is

Does Woo love you?

When we are apart, heartfelt thoughts continually trickle through

of you

I see you flying when happy.

You need to know how this thrills me and brings me glee.

Does Woo love you?

I beg never to miss the tenderness and sweetness of your kisses

in that dance of two, where the mystery of love has us as one.

Your countenance expresses that it's much more than fun.

In pleasure, you plead, "Stop, please don't stop…"

Please could it be,

that the woman who travailed

with my posterity

not be loved by me?

Verily, verily my poopie

I do, I do love thee.

Woo

Her Name is Grace

Therefore shall a man leave his father and his mother, and shall cleave unto his wife: and they shall be one flesh.

GENESIS 2:24 KJV

CHAPTER 1

Jejune Love

Jejune love is naive, simplistic, and superficial. And that is how I conceptualized affection of any kind. I inculcated my ideas within a home where the term 'love' did not appear to exist. My parents did not often speak those powerful words and the things they did for us were not understood as love in action until I was an adult.

I yearned to hear and feel the mysteries of what love afforded me. Still, unfortunately, my simple lifestyle and naivete found me amid a superficial love that veered in an unfamiliar direction. My ignorance and lack of relationship training caused me to see things through rose-colored glasses. I could smell the perfect air and see the house with the white picket fence, full of babies. Through those glasses, I also saw a relationship that would not deprive me of my desires. Perhaps I believed I was supposed to have that life—nothing less.

Jejune love, in its youthfulness, is the form of love that can make or break your future beliefs in the quintessential love of God. John 3:16 states, **"For God so loved the world that he gave his only begotten Son, that whosoever believeth in him shall not perish but have everlasting life."**

There is tremendous power in Love, as defined by God.

My Heavenly Father brought about the genesis of a love that was raw, fresh, powerful, and ever-so-tempting. Jejune love is sweet and delightful that way. In my inexperience, it was a danger to me. I lived a life full of excitement, joy, and happiness, only it was an illusion of grandiose plans.

I was searching and thought I found that kind of agape love that would carry us into the endless tomorrows. But because of this jejune love, I became a pawn of the enemy. His goal was to attempt to steer me away from my purpose, and initially, he appeared successful. But he did not understand that the detour he "orchestrated" was equipping me for the greater purpose God had planned for me. I had to learn that also.

Come away with me to the land of freedom and rose-colored glasses, where everything looks picture-perfect. You can fall into a space of time that reflects all your dreams and desires, and nothing harmful or destructive happens. That place where you and your perfect young man cannot see beyond what he wants or expects. Why? Because you believe love is giving yourself to another, even if it is, paradoxically, to your hurt!

Wait, Like Father Said

What are you going to do?

Can I be intimate with you?

Don't shake your head, no!

It's ok

He said

We are in love

I looked into his eyes and told him my whys

But that was not enough

He wanted me intimately

But I could not be rushed

I'm fifteen, I exclaimed

I must remain

Until I get a spouse

If you love me,

he pleaded

I'm down on my knees

Let me have you

He said

This once

I wrinkled my brow and shook my head

I must do what Father said

Wait until marriage
that is best
Keep yourself clean and not a mess
True love will come and is willing to wait
Be patient, my daughter
Time it will take

My Momma's Home

He's pressuring me almost every day

I don't want to

That's what I say

Stop pestering me. I want to be free

Free of this kind of intimacy

The time had come

The pressure was on

He wanted more of me

I told him no

It cannot be

He pressed some more

But wouldn't take no for an answer

He kept on asking

Can we be alone?

Not this time

My momma's home

Again, he came

With the same routine

I love you, and I need you

Can we be alone?

No, we can't!

I had to take a stance.

I was determined to be free.

Of any intimacy

Once again, he'd asked

Come on girl

You've got to do it sometime

So why not let it be with me

We are not married

So, leave me be

I don't want that kind of intimacy

Now he's angry, and I am getting sad

This is too much

Have I been had?

I know a girl, he said

Her Name is Grace

She will do all I ask

She loves me

I told her she couldn't have me

Because I'm not free

You see how much I love you

I turned her down

Because all I want to do

Is be with you

So, tell me

Can we be alone?

No

My momma's home

Patricia Johnson

Illusion

Slow and methodical

My heartbeat like the rhythm of a drum

Talking to someone

It was back when

In that time of naivete

Believing that happiness would last all-day

A dance we shared one time, long ago

The two become one

That's how it was done

Not knowing the consequences

It was all out of sight

Old enough to think we were right

Youthful love or infatuation as it was

A song of faith and joy

The love between a girl and a boy

Doing that dance of life

Her Name is Grace

One of promises and hope too

Expecting all of our dreams to come true

Playing husband and wife

We were too young to become one

Too young to understand it was wrong

Wanting the children, we hoped to gain

To complete our illusion

It only brought confusion

Nonetheless, it was done

And our life had just begun

Patricia Johnson

My Jewel

It was nighttime
8:45
The two of us alone, he and I

Babysitting the kids
No adults around
They were at the club downtown

So, I lay on the floor
Curiosity set in
And let him open the door

By nine, it was done
And it was not fun

I shake my head in wonder
I can't tell anyone!
I take a bath and sit on my bed
What's done is done

My jewel, so precious

Her Name is Grace

It can't be replaced

Gone forever in a moment of haste

The innocence of my youth

I can never regain

Oh, Father! I am so sorry

What a shame!

I did not listen to you

How could this be?

I am too young for this type of intimacy

Curiosity got to me

It took me for a ride

And I fell over the side

Forgive me!

Father, what have I done?

I have been intimate with someone.

Patricia Johnson

Broken

I lay dazed by the thought of you
I lay perplexed by the things you'd do

I bleed from the purity of what I had
Heartbroken petals lay upon my bed
My pure self
Now has been broken
You took it all

I allowed you to take me
The most intimate me
The fragileness of me
My inner me

I lay dazed by the thought of you
I lay perplexed by the things you'd do

The pain of your entering did not deter me
But my pain has not subsided with the exit of you
My petals slowly wilting from the hate of you

Her Name is Grace

You took, and I gave

You used and soiled

I thought it was love

Pure and clean

I gave all of me; I had nothing else

I lay dazed by the thought of you

I lay perplexed by the things you'd do

You lay in me, feeling me

Being one with me

Just to withdraw from me

After spilling your seed in me

Leaving me

In pain of heart, mind, and body

My flower slowly closed the folds that surround my honey

The sweetness of me that wanted you

I lay dazed by the thought of you

I lay perplexed by the things you'd do

Being one with me

Just to withdraw from me

After spilling seed in me

Patricia Johnson

In pain of heart, mind, and body

It wasn't worth it to me!

It's Just Sex

I call out your name.

You make my body pour out.

The delight of you

The intimacy with you

My body cries

But it's all lies

I ooh and ahh

But it means not a thing

It's sex

What next

More ooh and ahh

Oh, baby, here

Oh, daddy, there

It's all a farce

To appease your vanity

Help you think you have it all

Including the moves that make me ride

The imposter is out

My true self alone

In the shell of my body

Wanting to go home

I don't feel what you do

The aahhhs and the oohs

Oh, baby, here

Oh, daddy, there

And you think you're it!

It's all a farce to make you proud

Your manhood is fragile

The imposter is out

My true self alone

In the shell of my body

Wanting to go home

I don't feel what you do

The aahhhs and the oohs

It's just sex

But it's not

What ya gon' do

The Sensualness of Me

I stand and view myself in the mirror

Ashamed to peek at the mounds of my breast

Or the v that meets at my thighs

The sensualness of me is nothing to be ashamed of

The sensualness of me is nothing to be afraid of

The sensualness of me is not to be ridiculed or considered taboo

The sensualness of me is not his to explore

The sensualness of me gratifying the senses

Smell, taste, touch, see and hear

While exploring what makes me

I stand and view myself in the mirror

Ashamed to peek at the mounds of my breast

Or the v that meets at my thighs

Averting my eyes so that I don't offend

The girl that lay within

Ashamed to explore the reality of me

It's taboo to touch or acknowledge that I'm ripe

The shame causes the flame

The flushing of my face

Patricia Johnson

I stand and view myself in the mirror

Ashamed to peek at the mounds of my breast

Or the v that meets at my thighs

The shame I'm taught

Unleashed in me

Exposing my heart to such grief

The girl that lay within

To her chagrin

Cannot withstand the guilt

She covers herself

Averts her eyes and breathes a sigh of relief

I stand and view myself in the mirror

Ashamed to peek at the mounds of my breast

Or the v that meets at my thighs

Ashamed to explore the reality of me

It's taboo to touch or acknowledge that I have changed

The shame I'm taught

Unleashing in me

Strangling me

I'm at an impasse

The woman in me wants to see

To explore

But the girl in me refrained me

Shame is at the door

Patricia Johnson

Why must I?

Why must I be afraid?

To express my sensuality to myself.

Why must I be timid and shy?

To express my sensuality to myself.

Why must I pretend that what I feel and see does not exist?

Why must I swoon and blush at the rise and fall of my breast?

Why must I pretend that God's beauty didn't unfold?

I am a child becoming a woman, and fear has held me close

Too afraid to raise my brow at the awakening of the host

Feeling those desires that come with the kiss of a breeze

I've shed my naivete and innocence in the blood

Why must I be afraid?

To express my sensuality to myself.

Why must I be timid and shy?

To express my sensuality to myself.

Why must I pretend that what I feel and see does not exist

Why must I swoon and blush at the rise and fall of my breast?

Why must I pretend that God's beauty didn't unfold?

Why must I be afraid to express my sensuality to myself?

Why must I be afraid to express my sensuality to myself?

Why?

CHAPTER 2

The Strength of Learning and Loving Me

It has taken decades for the strength of love, unbeknownst to me, to come forth and shine as a beacon of hope. It was an arduous climb from the chasm in which I found myself entombed. Life had me faced down upon the cold, dark, dampness of the earth, lulling me into a stagnated existence. Beneath the weight of heartache, abuse, and the emptiness that continually drained the life from me, I was trapped.

I could not love myself. I could not fight for myself. I could not <u>find</u> myself because I did not know myself.

I lost my voice under the oppression of a jejune love that became my greatest misery. His was the iron fist of a young man who only knew the kind of affection expressed within his home, self-taught and violent. He inflicted his dark education upon my person and called it love. I didn't understand. But I learned well.

Viewing myself through those "rose-colored" glasses left me unprotected, fragile, and in pieces as days turned into months and years. Eventually, I was forced to look upon those fragments that used to be me and began to feel a sense of hopelessness.

How could I love me?

Look at me!

Her Name is Grace

How could I love what I had become?!

I spewed those words vehemently across the multifaceted reflections of me. The light reflecting upon the shards of my journey inflamed the scars, pain, hurt, disillusion, and hopelessness that lay at my feet. Dances began to stir within me; ones I could not withhold, and I began marking time over the most vulnerable pieces representing my totality. Melodies found me, some soft and as gentle as a summer breeze. Others were as odious as the chaotic symbols and brass that tantalized my battered soul. This fusion of sound was authentic, wholly my own, and unique to those very things that held me captive. They became a prolific piece that caused my mind to oscillate, my body to sway and my heart to swirl to the mysterious jazz reverberating within my heart. It was, finally, a dance that identified me and only me!

The smooth rhythm and blues took me back to the shores of the motherland we call Africa. And yet, I was still somewhat lost.

Finding me was not something simple, easy, or of certainty. It was not looking at my reflection in the mirror or taking a journey down memory lane. Instead, my healing journey encompassed losing myself, jarring scars to loosen their hold, and removing the blindfold so my vision could clear. I had to expose my heart to its own brokenness and turn to God for deliverance, renewal, refreshing, and safety. The work of my freedom included sorting through battles, losses, wins, and survival.

I was victorious.

Eventually.

And I am not done.

I am ever learning new dimensions, levels, and spaces that need to be discovered, refreshed, and at times destroyed.

Throughout the process, I know God has me, and He loves me. My self-love evolves because he first loved me, and I can say with a blessed assurance that my journey of discovery does not end here.

My Old Nature

My old nature tried to keep me down.

Causing me to become tremulous

It forever wants to keep me quiet

So my new nature is not heard

diffident

acquiescent

moving to the side

My new nature

in obscurity

buried deep

below the recesses of my mind

My old nature

impetuous and rash

wanting to drag me around

in my past

But the assiduous ardor of the new creature

continued to badger me

knocking at the door of my heart

begging for liberty

I had to do what I had to do!

I gave deference to the new

told the old goodbye

My new nature absolved me

I am free

Enough

For years I believed I was not

Enough

You told me I was not

Enough

You showed me I was not

Enough

Like a soldier, I was war-torn and battle fatigued

I fought to be

Enough

I tried to be

Enough

Still, I was not

Enough

Like a doll, I was pretty

But I was not

Enough

I lived off of what you spoke

Yet, I was not

Enough

You never said you loved me

Because I was not

Enough

I could not be in the company of others

I was not

Enough

Enough is Enough!

I am more than enough

I am enough for a man that loves me

I am enough to be single and free

I am enough to love who I am

I am enough

You are enough

Woman, stand up and know you are enough!

We are enough

Me

I am beginning to learn myself.

Through counseling and its theories

I can see who I was

I can see where I am

I can see where I need to be

I am free

My autonomy is mine

My decisions are fine

My self is in line with me

I am free

Free to be me

I did not get here in the twinkling of an eye

I did not have to wait to die

I did not have to walk in despair

I had to find myself to know I was free

Free to be me

I can look through the window of time

My liberty was lost

My freedoms were thrown about

I was a slave to my broken heart

Patricia Johnson

I had to get to know myself

I had to be free

Free to love me

But how can I love me

if I don't know me

Am I free

to be me

I have captured my youth.

Through the eyes of my now

I have emptied myself of the pains from my past

Self-pity, passivity, and those things I fought

I let it go

I learned to extricate myself

In time I was free

Free to be me

My journey is not over

And I am alive

I live on purpose

Intentionally making choices

Intentionally being free

Intentionally being

Me

No

He stood behind me and grabbed me at my waist

"I love you"

He whispered those words in haste

I almost believed as he nibbled my ear

But I stayed in control and said,

"No, My dear.!"

I am not yours to grab, hold or caress

I am not yours to love on request

I am my own woman, and I choose

not to part

with any of me

I see the colors you possess

No!

Not me!

He stood behind me and grabbed me at my waist

"I love you"

He whispered those words in haste

I almost believed as he nibbled my ear

I was in control and said,

"No, my dear!"

Patricia Johnson

I am not the one to be taken for granted

I am not the one to be led by lust

I am not the one who needs you

I am in control

I am my own woman

And I said

"NO!"

Maidenhood

My maidenhood lay nestled at the center of me

That part of me safe and secure

I will not allow another to casually see

For it is too special to treat callously

Too rich to throw away

Too fresh to spoil

Too valuable to allow you to have

Neither to taste nor touch

That very special part of me

My maidenhood lay nestled at the center of me

That part of me safe and secure

I will not allow another to cavalierly see

It is pure

It is priceless

My jewel

My richness

The value of me

The authenticity of me

My maidenhood lay nestled at the center of me

In my chest of treasures

Patricia Johnson

Undisturbed

But for one to see

One to taste, touch, and love

Right now

It is just for me.

Sherry

My sherry is as sweet as the best wine

As intoxicating as the strongest drink

I know you would like to

part and taste

Your haste to have

turned me off

You flirt and fumble

words at a loss

You want to get lost

in me

See my inner rose

Taste of me

Have your way with me

My sherry is as sweet as the best wine

As intoxicating as the strongest drink

I will not depart from her

It doesn't matter

what you try

how you seek

Patricia Johnson

My winery

My still

It is closed to all

But for that man

The one that cometh on bended knee

The one that will hold my hand and ask

The one who will seek my "Yes"

That man, the one I marry

He will taste the goodness of my sherry

Marry Me

He walked up behind me.

Pressing his strength into the warmth of me

Wrapping his arms gently around me

The firmness of him causing me to stir

I glance up at him and fall into his eyes

They are hypnotic

I am mesmerized

Drinking in the desire of him

Closing my eyes

I feel him stir yet again

My lips part at the thought of him

Holding me tighter

His manhood grows

But

As I have told myself

I am not ready

Repeating the mantra

I am afraid

I have not done this in a while

I don't know what he might expect

from someone such as me

Patricia Johnson

I am older, yet my experience is lacking

I feel like a young maiden

nervous and inhibited

I tilt my head back to rest on his shoulder

His member

gaining in strength

I am still hesitant

I look up and search his eyes once again

I want to lose myself in the center of him.

But

I can not

I should not

I will not

It is too soon

His body is calling me

He spoke no words

His eyes beckoned me to release

my honey, my sweetness, my heat

My sensual self

All of me

He wants me

He can taste it, feel it

he believes he sees it

But, I tell him, "No!"

Her Name is Grace

If you want all that I have

My honeycomb, my heat, my tightness, my sweet

My sensual self

To taste me, to feel me,

To become one with me

To have all of me

You must marry me

Patricia Johnson

Fortissimo

I have found my voice

I am a woman

I have found my voice

In the recess of myself

I have found my voice

I am a woman

My voice is no longer silent

No longer quiet

No longer afraid

My voice, no longer shrill

No shrieking distortion

It is now clear

Precise

Strong

Fortissimo

My voice

Ringing with clarity

The force

Her Name is Grace

The power

The strength

Fortissimo

My voice

No longer a gentle breeze

A droplet of rain or leaves falling from trees

I am a woman

Fortissimo

My voice is a beacon in the night

My voice is as the roaring seas

My voice is thunder and lightning across the skies

I am a woman

Fortissimo

My voice lives

My voice thrives

My voice does not hide

I am a woman

Fortissimo

My voice is significant

Quintessential

Intrinsic

Natural

Necessary

I am a woman

Fortissimo

CHAPTER 3

Revealed Love

Revealed love allows one the freedom to open and expose their heart. This idea of giving all of myself to another was not one I could initially accept. I believed the mistrust and stiffness of my unwillingness could not be carved through, not after the disappointments and heartbreak of my Jejune love.

I was full of tremendous angst.

I could only imagine what it would feel like to have someone in my life that would intentionally listen to my heart. The rhythm of its beat was irregular and no longer held a clear or healthy pattern. When I attempted to center on exposing and revealing my inner being, my heart skipped. The pain was so substantial that the very idea of allowing anyone entrance caused immense trepidation. As a result, my heart would race.

I had become encapsulated within the confines of self-doubt, and insecurity. Prisoner was I to thwarted love, controlling love, and, worst of all, the demeaning love I continually turned upon myself.

But then a man, a beautiful Black man, entered my life.

He was one I finally believed I could give my heart to. I felt free to lay it at his feet with the assurance that he would never crush it. He was that particular person who accepted my entire self and <u>courted</u> me. I knew this man was different; his truth was precisely that, no additions, or subtractions. This melanin-filled man proved himself to be the one who would never attempt to change me. His desire was only to enhance me.

As I did him.

This revealed love was still relatively new and challenging. But through the strength of Christ loving me (and me beginning to fully engage in loving me), I began to understand one thing.

I could not live in fear.

I could not continue to participate with fear that I would be rejected or poorly treated. I had to use the wisdom I received and live on purpose. I had to allow my growth to live and thrive and allow the poignant reminders of my past to die.

Scripture states that **"we walk by faith, not by sight"** (**2 Corinthians 5:7**).

I had to believe that God would allow me to be a good thing to that man who found this redeemed, revived me. I had to think that God would allow this man to expose himself in a way to which I could respond with trust. I believed God would allow this man to reveal his heart, vulnerabilities, and authentic self.

I had to believe it!

Nescient

I quietly cry with my head upon my pillow

Sleep does not appear to visit

She alludes me

I desperately seek her out

She does not respond

I search for her

I need her

Where could she be?

Nescient

I look into the blackness of night.

My pain mingles with the cold air

With the deep despair

Sadness leaves me no peace.

The grandeur of this moment spirals

amid the perplexing emotions that have begun to fill me.

I am walking

I am turning

I am stumbling

I am falling into the abyss of nothingness

Patricia Johnson

Nescient

A gentle flower not yet full bloomed
The rain gently fell upon her moon
The stars no longer dancing
The light is dim
The horizon is bleak
The trees speak in the gentle breeze
Branches swaying, dancing
Interweaving with my mood
The stillness a facade of the night

Nescient

I quietly cry
my head upon my pillow
Sleep does not appear to visit
She alludes me
I desperately seek her out
She does not respond
I search for her
I need her
Where could she be?

Nescient

As I look into the blackness of night
My pain mingles with the cold air
With the deep despair
Sadness that leaves me no peace.
The grandeur of this moment spirals
amid the perplexing emotions that have begun to fill me.
I am walking
I am turning
I am spinning
I am stumbling
I am falling into the abyss of nothingness

Nescient

Her flower
Dimmed from the night

The kiss of the Son

Her petals unfold
She has opened

Patricia Johnson

Her glory shines

She is with our Father

In whom she now resides

Hallelujah

Angels rejoice

But

Nescient

While I quietly cry

my head upon my pillow

Sleep does not appear to visit

As I look into the blackness of night

My pain mingles with the cold air

With the deep despair

With sadness that leaves me no peace.

The grandeur of this moment

spirals

amid the perplexing emotions

filling me.

I am walking

I am turning

Her Name is Grace

I am spinning

I am stumbling

Falling

into the abyss of nothingness

Nescient

I do not understand

Patricia Johnson

My Darling Man

You say that you love me, and I can tell you all.

Without judgment, scorn, or half-listening

I am ready, my darling, to pour out my heart

To allow you the true me, all of me

It is not easy to open this door

Unlike you, I have done this before

But

It backfired

And then knocked me to the floor

I told him all and received his contempt

Your love for me is more than we had

So, I peel back the layers

Expose my heart

I want you to see and understand me

It all began when I was young;

I did not love him.

I wanted someone to listen

Share things I had never done

And in time become one

He hurt me badly, so badly I wanted to die

And at times, I tried to end it

Her Name is Grace

But God would not have it

We were together a long time

when he asked the question

"Will you marry me?"

I was afraid to say no

I lived a life of humiliation and degradation

Physical, mental, and emotional abuse

Pain so intense I could not breathe

Fleeing was not an option

Fear made me freeze

in that spot

He beat me, strangled me

verbally assaulted me

So, I decided on a cold November night

to stop the abuse

I was tired, frustrated

scared out of my mind

walking through a fog of pain and misery

that night in '93

I ended my husband's life

I am not a mad black woman

I am just me

A woman with a lot of history

I had to tell you this to set me free.

Patricia Johnson

Please do not judge me

Or think I am crazy

I wanted to survive

Live

Not die

I will not live a life of guilt

Nor hold my head down in shame

I will not live, trying to hide my past

Or harboring any more pain

I stand before you in my nakedness

Exposing all of me

I am who I am

Accept me

or leave me

that is your choice

But I decided to allow the layers to open

Suffer the truth to bleed forth

To let you in

and set myself free

His Response

My darling woman, your past is your past

I do not judge

I am a man of my word

I will not throw in your face things that you have done

Or what has been done to you

I will not abuse, ridicule,

hurt you

or inflict pain upon you

My love is unconditional, adhesive, and concrete

My love for you is not a game of hurt and pain

My love for you is the sweet smell of a rose

A sunrise, hope, joy, and happiness

My love for you is caring for you, protecting you,

and honoring you

It shall never fade or become weak

My love for you wants all of you

Your weakness, your strength, your gentleness

It surpasses all I desire

It is not selfish or blind

to whom you are

My love is unconditional, adhesive, and concrete

My love for you is not a game of hurt and pain

My love is the love of God

for you!

Despite what you have done

My love is genuine

Am I Good Enough

People look at me

say that I am not enough

You chose me

I do not understand why

There is nothing extraordinary about me

No specialty

No beauty

I am not 5'7, slim, and trim

I am not athletic or go to the gym

Your family cannot see

why you chose me

I was a battered wife

For ten years I lived this life

I tried to hide the shame within

Killing my spouse was a sin

Shame shrouded my heart and mind

But you chose me

I cannot see

Patricia Johnson

I don't understand
Why me?

I am insecure
I have physical, mental
and emotional scars
They run deep
My issues are painful to keep

My emotional state is out of this world
I ride on high
Feeling sad the next moment
hopeless and empty
Insomnia is part of me
Sleep resists me
Worthless I must be
Bipolar
maybe

He beat me
Feeling guilty and carrying my shame
I can't face my family
They know my name
Euphoria, irritability

Her Name is Grace

Exhausted to death

revved up and on the move

Bipolar keeps me going

This roller coaster never stops

Bipolar

maybe

But you chose me

I don't feel that I am good enough

Or live up to what you expect

You don't understand

the things that brought me here

Neither do you condescend

Or make me feel less than

You chose me

I don't understand

There is nothing extraordinary about me

No specialty

No beauty

I'm not 5'7 slim and trim

I am not athletic or go to the gym

I am a woman

whose been broken

beaten and battered

I am a woman who was lost in the storm

A fragmented heart that only God can fix

A woman who carries the pain

of her whole life before you

Bipolar

maybe

Why did you choose me?

His Response

I chose you

My heart compelled me to

I chose you

Because of your pain

I chose you

Because of your beauty

I see how God views you

Your brokenness

Your shame

Through the lens of fearfully and wonderfully made

I chose you

To love you

Help you

Pray for you

To care for your heart and help you mend

I chose you

God showed me your pain and your hurt

He showed me the secrets that lay within

Your broken places, fragmented pieces

and hollow halls of your heart

He allowed me to hear the echoes of your yearnings

The pleas of silent help that coursed through your dreams

I chose you

When I espied you

God said, "She is the one."

He knows your past, your pain, all that you have endured

Bipolar maybe

So what?

Love covers

The roller coaster you are on

The storm

You will go through

The winds will be fierce

The waters will rise

The lighting will strike

Her Name is Grace

Your life

Upheaval

Turmoil

Chaos

Pandemonium

A cataclysmic event

Your pain will come forth

And I will be with you

I love you

Your world was torn

Ripped from your grasp

The hole in your heart as wide as the sea

But consider

The torrential rains

helped you

break free

It won't be easy

but you will get through

I am here to help you

You are God's daughter

I am his son

He told me you were the one

Patricia Johnson

You

Are

Enough

Size and Shape

Why do I hide from you?

I can't undress before you

I know that I have gained sixty pounds

My weight is not fake

I feel ashamed

My hourglass figure

The hips that you adored

Nowhere to be seen

Food has transformed me

My mental state caused this issue

I eat and eat to absolve my pain

But I awaken mortified by my sin

The food I idolize causes me to hide

For as much as I love you

I can not

Undress before you

Lights must be off

The shades down

The curtains drawn

Patricia Johnson

This burden is heavy

And yes, I love you

But

I cannot undress before you

How can you love me?

I am as heavy as can be

I see myself in the mirror

Rolls and rolls

layers, and layers

Stomach protruding

And yet,

I do care!

I want to find the woman you fell in love with

The woman you married

Life has been hard

Feelings and emotions I could not control

My pain, my problem

I would not dare

open that door

Would you listen?

Would you care?

Her Name is Grace

I cannot undress before you

I am ashamed

I lost who I was

And I can feel the pain

Layers and layers of emotional distress

How could I share my unhappiness?

I dove into my past and looked to see

I was eating to be free

Steak subs, fries, cookies, cakes, and pies

Chicken wings, and all those things

I could not resist

My mind was not my own

After I partook of all that food for the flesh

I could do no more than look at the floor

Need I say more!

Why do I hide from you?

I can't undress before you

How can you love me?

I am sixty pounds heavier

I can't love myself

What does that tell you?

Patricia Johnson

I try hard to eat to live

but my love affair with food has taken a grip

The fork clasped in my hand

I cannot let go

It feels so good to me

The immediate gratification

Adoration

My idol

Why do I hide from you?

I can't undress before you

I know it doesn't belong

How do I get back to Abba?

Back to my Father through Christ

How do I put the fork down

and give Him my life?

I am living to eat

Not eating to live

Why do I hide from you?

I can't undress before you

I found so much pleasure

In the drug of my choice

How do I let go and be free?

Free of the idol in me

Her Name is Grace

His Response

My darling wife

Your size and shape are not an issue for me

Never has been and never will be

I love you as you are

Any shape or size

8, 10, 14, 18 or 22

I will always love you

When I look at you

I admire you

and desire to touch you

I am feeding upon the Spirit in you

My love is concrete; hard and sure

My love for you is not contingent on your size, shape

or mental state

I give my love freely

unapologetically, unashamedly, and unconditionally

I love every inch of you

Every part of you

I see the glory of you the beauty of you

My eyes are focused beyond the physical

I see you

from the place my Father does

Fearfully and wonderfully made

My darling wife

I don't understand the cause of your pain

but together on our knees, we will gain

Knowledge to fight so healing can begin

I will hold you, comfort you,

stand by you, guide you

fast for you

continually

stay on my knees praying for you

I love you as Christ so loves the church

I will lay down all for you

You are my wife, my heart, my good thing

size and shape do not matter to me

Your well-being

State of mind

Emotions

Physical and spiritual health

THAT

Is important to me

You in totality

Your whole self

My love, you are significant

Important

and worthy of my attention

I promise you

I will never leave you

Berate you or talk down to you

I am here to stand by you

Protect you

and yes

To love you

Patricia Johnson

Four-Letter Word

I have been struggling

The food I eat

Killing me

Holding me

Daring me

I have been struggling

Unable to see clearly

Unable to hear

Unable to move

Unable to breathe

I have been struggling

The test of time

My table before me

The meats of Pharaoh

I have been struggling

Putting the tools of the trade away

I dare say

I have not

Her Name is Grace

I have been struggling
The fork, spoon, knife, and plate
It appears we are always on a date

The movies, home, or with my friends
I am not alone
It's always there
I'm struggling

I view myself in the reflecting glass
I see stress, anxiety
and too much of me

I view myself in the reflecting glass
Excess weight
Diabetes
Hypercholesterolemia
Hair loss
Tired
It is true
I did this to you

I view myself in the mirror

Painted face

Without a trace

Of myself

Trying to hide

From the look of you inside

Heart-healthy and strong

Blessed

None-the-less

I have been struggling

Is it, my enemy

The thoughts within

My mind fighting a battle

I can't win

My enemy

The one who seeks me

Out to destroy me

I am struggling

Need I say more

Anxiety and stress

They can attest

Her Name is Grace

My enemy

One who seeks me

Out to destroy me

My nemesis

Kryptonite

haunting me

Power in his arsenal

To destroy me

The power over me is intense

It is magnified each day

I open my eyes and what do I hear?

A four-letter word

It is killing me

Yet, I cannot live without it

My attraction is strong

The pull, hard and tight

It is killing me

The yoke that has me bound

Enslaved and asleep

I am weak

Patricia Johnson

It is killing me

That four-letter word
Mystifies me
Enthralls me
Romances me
Loves me
And wants every inch of me

That four-letter word
I need to survive
Yet I am surviving for more

YOU four-letter word
I want to stop loving you
I hate you
I want to evict you
Annihilate you
Rid myself of you
I don't need you

Yet,
I am enraptured by you

Her Name is Grace

The whispers of you

The smell of you

The look of you

The taste of you

To become one with you

You are always on my mind

Why can't I control you?

Four letter word

You are small yet powerful

Your pull is ever there

How do I dare?

I want to hurt you

But I need you

I want to live without you

But I need you

I want to

My body needs to

My mind has to

My tongue excited to

Four letter word

Patricia Johnson

I must move on

I must give you up

Not completely

But come at you differently

Four letter word

Things can never be the same

I was living to have you

You were my thing

But now,

He has prepared the table

before mine enemies

I eat from the Master's table

I hunger and thirst after righteousness

A crumb that falls will sustain me

Living water from my belly will flow

Four letter word

You must go!

My Trauma

My man spoke to me...

Get a little closer

I want to feel the warmth of you

Look at me

my love

I want to capture you

Your attention is what I need

I see the tears you try to hide

Always when you are close to me

What's bothering you?

Please tell me

I don't want you hurt

I don't want you depressed

You are not alone

Please tell me, my love?

Let me in

Don't push me aside

There is nothing you have to hide

My thoughts...

I am trying to hide

Patricia Johnson

My tears fall upon my pillow

My underlying trauma

Reaching from within

Something I cannot face

It's affecting my marriage

but what will he do?

Can I release it and expose the cause

Share my agony

Will it make him change?

Will this marriage end?

I cannot trust myself to speak

I am feeling very weak

What should I do?

My prayer to God...

I pray to God that he takes my hand

That he lifts it to his lips

gently kiss my fingertips

I need assurance to release my pain

Can I trust him, Father?

Will he continue to love me

Or play the game of love and hate

Can he be true?

Not to me

But to you

I love him with all I possess

But...

My love for you Father is matchless

No love can compare or captivate my heart

His is close

But is he on the mark?

My man, solicitous...

My love, my little lady he called

He looked into my eyes the depth of my soul

Patricia Johnson

He searched me

Captivated me

His gaze never left me

As he lifted my left hand

and kissed the tips of my fingers

He smiled at me and said he loved me

Encouraging me to release the trauma within

He looked desperate

But he continued to hold my hand

Watching

Waiting

Expecting a response

No judgment

Only care and concern

God prepared me…

I gave all …

To you my God

I give you praise

You answered my call

and now I am brave

He is the one

He did as I asked

My petition came to pass

I told…

I took a deep breath

And exhaled slowly

I looked at him and told him

My trauma you don't know

I was a child

Left alone when the man was home

He turned to me

And asked to see

All of me

I was young so very young

My eyes had never beheld such fear

How could he?

Desire to know me

Patricia Johnson

I screamed

I yelled

I kicked

I fought

He was stronger

But I continued my battle

He pressed me

Entered me

Soiled me

And left me

My body curled like a baby in the womb

A deluge of tears that could not be staunched

In the midst of my innocence, I lost

Affliction and emptiness began to reside

My mind was afire with the agony of this event

I could not comprehend the magnitude of this deed

Oh, God why?

Why did this man hurt me?

He took from me

Defiled me

Debased me

Destroying me

Pushing me into self

A place of isolation, darkness, and cold

I cannot see, hear, feel or think

I have been swallowed by the evil of man

I cried out to God and asked him why?

Why did you allow this to happen?

I could not understand

The blood is on his hands

I gave my life to Christ long before

Why was I not protected?

Jesus died so I may live

Yet on that night

I lost my life to the whims of the enemy

Held captive

by the bonds that still won't release me

I could not move

I was paralyzed

I was lost inside of me

He listened…

My man continued to give me his ear

I continued...

I know you want to hear it all

But understand the difficulty with which I speak

Opening my heart is tender, it hurts

But I want to be free

It's hard to look you in the eyes

Judged or despised

I am afraid to see

Behind the depths of thee

I longed to let this go

And still, I do not understand

Why didn't God take my hand and protect me?

Why was my innocence allowed to be stripped away?

No longer a little girl who wants to go play

My dolls, blocks, bikes, and games

No friends or family

I can't blame

Perhaps it was me

Were my skirts too high and shirts too tight

My breast in bloom

Could that be?

I don't understand Lord!

Why me?

My man, my darling black man

Please don't turn away.

Please don't leave me.

Will you stay?

My black man responds …

My lovely, lovely lady

I will stand by you

I will pray for you

I will continue to love you

Accept you

Protect you

And dare to cover you

God **never** left you

He understands you

What you have been through

Was not your fault

You were innocent

A child

A maiden

A ewe lamb

I don't understand why this happened to you

But I do know God truly loves you

Patricia Johnson

Your pain is not lost but attests to your strength

I am sorry my love that you suffered this thing

Your trauma, your body, mind, and spirit will heal

God will see that you are set free

The bonds and chains that hold you

Is beginning to release you

I am here to help you

Show you

Regardless of what you went through,

I am here for you

I explained before that my love is true

My love is concrete, real, and not superficial

I love you dear lady

With all of my heart

Your burden is mine

we carry it together

With our faces to the floor and Jesus at the door

God will allow us entrance and freedom will reign

Liberty will come

Whilst we walk by faith

Can you see the victory?

Don't allow your past to continue to haunt you

Don't be afraid

Let go

Let God

Let me

Love you.

Patricia Johnson

I Am Still Standing

I am still standing

My back is straight
My head is held high
I am still standing

My stature is sure
My posture steadfast
Comported
Poised
Equanimity
All in line with me

I am still standing

Value
Worth
Substance
Essence
Unparalleled

Her Name is Grace

I am still standing

Exceptional

Unique

Mannerism

All mine

I am defined

I am still standing

CHAPTER 4

New Love

I have at last removed the veil that covered my vision during my jejune love phase. It has been a real blessing to expose my naivete and the simplistic view of love that I held to delve into retrospection and healing. Although jejune love became a road of many valleys, hills, pitfalls, and, at times, a broken spirit, it was a walk I had to take.

This walk foreshadowed my stepping into the arena of self-love and exposing my lack. I had to reveal my vulnerabilities to myself and look into my past to determine my present and plot my future. It was vital for me to come to terms with not loving myself so I could face the difficulties of accepting love from another.

I can love myself through God's grace and never-ending mercies. And I am learning to view myself as God views me. Through the microscopic lens of God, I can finally see that I am fearfully and wonderfully made. I came to fully understand that I am loveable, that I can love, and that I should not be afraid to shed my past worries and concerns. But first, I had to permit myself to love myself and cast out those spoken words that tried to destroy me.

Then, I had to minister to myself.

New love is not simplistic, naïve, or superficial. It is a love I have allowed to change me; one I walk into freely. It is a transforming love that brings me closer to the character of Christ.

I understood the possibility of getting hurt was present. However, I have embraced the grace to accept the things I cannot change and change the things I can. Through the eyes of God and the touch of his hand, I removed the imposters within and let my true self bloom unhindered. A man who loved me nurtured this blooming God's way, Agape.

Patricia Johnson

A Love Letter to God

I have fallen in love with you, yet again

My God, I am hidden within you

I hear your heart and feel the love of you

I have fallen in love yet again

I do not have to do anything to receive it

The love I cannot hide from, run from, or lose

Freely given

I have fallen in love yet again

You are not a man that you sin

Your heart is full of love, tenderness, compassion, and truth

Your love song to me is sweeter than sweet

You call me precious and tell me

I am

fearfully and wonderfully made

Your love is all-consuming

I am burning

and yearning

for you

I am enthralled by the thought of you

I have fallen in love yet again

You are my love

Her Name is Grace

You are my joy

My heartbeat

My peace

You are my kindness

A force to behold

Your love is true

I exist

Complete through you

The one on the cross

The Sacrificial Lamb

The Prince of Peace

Complete

I have fallen in love yet again

Patricia Johnson

The Balcony

He looked into my eyes and gently reached for my hand

I gazed upon the face of a magnificent creature

My Black man

Strong

Vulnerable

It does not detract from who he is

He becomes more human

more sensitive to being

with the exposure of his heart.

My man searched me longingly as we walked to the bottom of the stairs

We paused a moment as he brushed a light kiss upon my lips

The sun beginning to peek above the horizon

He was taking me to see something I had never seen before

He told me that he loved me

but there was a lot more

His love, he said, did not begin or end in the marriage bed

His passion, he said, was genuine

His love surpassed all that I could ever imagine or think love could be

Clasping my fingers in his, we began our assent

The stairs were steep, but I did not care

Her Name is Grace

My man had me

He loved me

Step by step, we began our journey together

I could see the top of the stairs and a pair of doors

and as we took that last step

he gently pulled me to him.

He turned me to face those vast doors

and very slowly

we began moving closer

closer

then he reached the handles and pulled

The doors opened upon a scene that paralyzed me

In the midst was a table filled;

cheese, crackers, grapes, wine,

and dainty hors d'oeuvres.

A delicacy for a queen.

My man watched as I surveyed the table.

My eyes beheld the gold chalice atop a white lace tablecloth

Golden candelabras, the centerpiece

The breeze causes the flames to flicker

Two white chairs facing the sun

The wonderment why he would go to such lengths to please me

Surprised me,

I had no words

He continued his gaze upon my face until he espied my tears

Gently he turned me to face him

Looking down from his height, he placed a finger beneath my chin and tilted my head upward

So, he could see clearly the tears running free down my cheeks

"Why do you cry, my love?"

I looked into those eyes so loving and true

But everything about him was new

The scene he played out before me

The food, the wine, the ambiance

even the temperature was right

all so perfect, my heart began to expand

What was he doing to me?

Was this a game?

One that I would

Like so many times before

lose

At that moment, a torrent of tears began to fall.

He did not release me from his hold and began to kiss my tears away

gently

"Why do you cry, my love?

Am I hurting you in some way?

Are they tears of joy?

Her Name is Grace

Tell me, my love, give me your heart, your joys, pains, or sorrows

What can I do for you?"

He whispered in my ear, "Tell me, love.

I want to hear your story.

I would never hurt you.

I am a man of my word.

To see you cry tugs at my heart

To know you are in pain grieves my soul

What is it, little one?

Please share your heart with me

Let us begin our relationship free

You are free to be!"

Taking a deep breath, I lay my head upon his chest

I could feel the beating of his heart

my worries began to fade

Gently and lovingly, he caressed my face

I hesitantly looked into his strong countenance

filled with compassion and strength

I hesitated yet again, in awe of him

My Black man

The man who loves me shed a tear

It traced the contours of his firm jaw

becoming lost within his beard

I knew this precise moment

was the moment

I would freely give my heart

But

Fear began to rattle me, move me, to a place of uncertainty

I have never known a man like him

He has shaken the very foundation of me

The stability in me

And yes, that frightened me

My tears began again as my eyes swept the scene.

My love, my darling man, you are more than a dream come true

I am shaking, from fear or joy I do not know

I turned from him in a swirl and allowed my hands to reminisce

The old man began to rise within me

Why?

Uncertainty, fear, past hurts, and pains

God, why? I thought these issues were resolved

Why is my mind at war and causing me to pause?

The sun and the moon orbit in unison

Caused my thoughts to gyrate and press upon me

The pressure so fierce I became unstable, and my mouth began to
speak

Without conscious volition, words began to run free

Her Name is Grace

Flowing over my tongue between my teeth and forward, they sprung

"What do you want from me?

I am not a beauty and have nothing to offer

Is it sex?

Is that the reason for this?!"

Tiny words landed at his feet; ones I dare not repeat.

My man placed his hands around my waist

and gently

yet intentionally

turned my back to him.

We breathed together

inhale, exhale, and breathe once more

in the distance, the waves hitting the shore

He forced me to see the beauty as it was

No hidden agenda, no debt to score

He spoke no words

The stillness of him disturbed by his breath

He held me close, so close we could have been one

He wrapped his arms tightly around me and kept me

Comforted me

calmed me

and poured love

upon me

He would not release me

He had to speak his peace

"Listen to me, my little one, and hear me well

I must reassure you

enlighten, and soothe you

Harken to my voice as I calm your apprehensions

I would never use, abuse, or intentionally hurt you

Nor would I curse you, mock, or make fun of you

My love is free, and it will never try to change or manipulate you

I will honor you, teach you, uplift, and encourage you

My love will allow you to be you

It is patient, kind, generous, and appreciative of what you offer

My love is not shallow; it is not fleeting

it is not contingent upon what you do

I want all of you, not bits and pieces

The authentic you

Because

I love you."

The Love of a Man

The love of a man for his woman

Defies what is normal

considered reasonable

There is no reasoning when true love prevails

There are no thoughts of life without that special woman

A love so fierce and on fire

he would climb the highest mountains

for her

He would swim the deepest seas

to comfort her

He would love her

in a way that makes her heart skip a beat

Causing butterflies to flitter and float in her tummy

He would bring out the best in her

Even her flaws

A pleasure

I must say

His love is forever

Indulging her with the desires of her heart

Not spoiling her

Encouraging her

Patricia Johnson

You are his sensibilities, his woman

He lost them long ago

To the love of his life

The woman he took as wife

Cosmos

I look into the beauty of you

And I espy Jesus

Your heart is giving and full of grace

Your walk is humble yet sure

You are going about your business

confident and steadfast

I look into the beauty of you

and I espy Jesus

Praying, fasting, and communing with God

Our cosmoses collide

The brilliance of the light

The dancing of the stars

The solar system of my love

Orbiting your moon

I am your Venus

I am blinded and off-balance by the power of you

My heart is racing

Unable to be still

The magnificence of the spectacle

Your glory

Piercing my senses

Patricia Johnson

I am falling into your space

Our joined cosmos

Reeling from the impact

Falling

Losing my way

The light, the brightness of it

My cosmos

lost within you

A cataclysmic union

fused with the beauty of you

The glory of you coming through

The God in you

piercing my soul

I revel in your beauty, power, and strength

I marvel at your glory

The majesty and pull have drawn me to you

Like a bee in the honeycomb

The sweet nectar that attracts

Our cosmos enjoined

Now I am part of you

God, Jesus, and Holy Spirit

God, I am illuminated by the shining presence of you

My being

Personified by the presence of your Spirit

The Comforter

He is my help

My conscious

He is my compass

My awareness

He leads me to You

He is a portion of You

Left behind to show me which way is You

Jesus

The sacrificial lamb

He taught us

Walked among us

Died for us

He rose

He sits

He lives

I live

I am free

In him

To become the woman that is

Me

My Man's Love

My man loves me

He is not defined by me

Nor I him

He indulges me

I do not whine, pout,

or cry because I did not have my way

I accept what he has to offer

I thank him every time

Not through sex or other forms of intimacy

But other things he needs from me

Faithfulness, kindness,

gentleness, and praise

He is a considerate man

Who loves me anyway

I am not perfect

Far from it

I cannot cook, bake,

or clean very well

But he loves me

My flaws and all

He accepts who I am

And does not want me to descend

He loves me

and persistently, consistently,

shows me

Through his thoughtfulness, love, and compassion

For being me and what I have to offer

He does not try to change me

Hurt me, or ridicule me

His love is not painful

does not defile, shame

nor is it selfish

His love nourishes, strengthens

brings out the best in me

My man is a man

Self-assured, fierce, and protective of my soul

He protects me from those things we see

He is on bended knees

daily

pleading the Blood over me

He loves me like Christ so love the church

Giving all for me

This love is profound

Her Name is Grace

It is beyond the here and now

When he looks at me

I feel

His tenderness, his kindness

Powerful

This man of mine

Genuinely loving

He is gentle in his lovemaking

Concurrently intense and extreme

His love, his kisses, his entering

Becoming one

United in Christ

My spirit soars, twists, and turns

My man and I entwined

Giving all of himself

Our bed undefiled

Our love, far more than sex

greater than a mere joining of two

I receive it

Our connection

in the spaciousness of time

floats above, beneath, and through the cosmos of heaven

Becoming one united and true

We are married, this man and me

Patricia Johnson

Before God, we stood

pledged a love He understood

Together forever, Christ our foundation

Our rock, shield, and our fortress

Substantial

We did not play with the oaths we proclaimed

Standing before God and giving our hearts

Promising to walk in purpose, Abba as our guide

My man is the person, husband,

and Father God called him to be

He leads his family in the word and is loved endlessly

I am in subjection

honoring my spouse

Uplifting him, encouraging him,

believing that he can

His love conveys commitment and faith

transferring passion

A voracious love

held dear

Why would we fear?

A Date

It was a beautiful day

Early morning, I should say

The breeze was cool

The sun was warm

God's glory fresh

from last night's storm

The trees, the sky, the clouds

The beauty of it all

What grandeur to behold

My man, my Black man

arrived at my door

The morning dew fresh upon his shoes

as he gained entrance into our home

Yelling out to me, a voice raspy and coarse

So Familiar

I knew

He was here

I ran to the door quickly

beheld the beauty of my spouse

Patricia Johnson

His smile

His joy

caused the butterflies to flitter

My goodness he is fine

This lovely Black man of mine

He kissed my forehead and looked into my eyes

His joy contagious, my laughter unrestrained

He caught me up in his arms nuzzling my neck

pouring on the charm

Hello, my wife, the love of my life, today is a day of freedom and play

He said

Never a week gone by where I am not amazed

The things he does, his generosity

selflessness displayed

Showing me love in so many ways

His love

I could not help but trust

The thought of him

Still causes me to blush

The heat rises and I am flushed

Tears of joy cloud my eyes

I have never experienced this before

This man, my man

My Black man

Her Name is Grace

He knows no boundaries with me

I cannot believe all that he does

From the bijou that I cherish

to petition Abba on my behalf

He is more than a man

that loves me

covers me

His outlook on life rests in Jesus

How could I ever despair?

My man

my Black man

my spouse

Not only does he have a kind heart

His heart and mine beat together

We are in sync

We are as one

Patricia Johnson

My Spouse

I walk to the bed and watch as he sleeps

The gentle rise and fall of his chest

The breath of life pulled into his lungs

Gently inhaled and expelled

The sweet sound of his breathing

always lulled me into a quiet slumber

Safety and security in the comforts of his arms

My man

my spouse

I reach out and glide my hand gently across his brow

Softly as not to awaken my love

Feelings of blessed assurance begin to rise

Overwhelmed with the look and feel of him

The totality of him

Never a raised utterance toward me

or a hand against me

Never disrespecting nor quieting my voice

Never allowing another to belittle or defame his wife

Protecting me,

gently scolding me

Her Name is Grace

Defending me

My Black man

my spouse

He is strong and attentive

He works hard and confronts challenges I know not of

He is a provider, lover, and friend

He allows the peace of God to reside within

My Black man, I am his queen

A hand of humility, justice, and truth

My authentic self-radiates from the love for him

My voice is heard

I do not have to yell

My cries eased with an embrace

My husband, lover, and friend

My king

My Black man

my spouse

Patricia Johnson

He is my Man

My man, my Black man

the one I adore

His strength lies far beyond the lovemaking we share

It is in the thoughtfulness and giving of spirit

the things that he does

Providing for his family and other families too

At times my bed is empty

the imprint of his head upon his pillow

Although his body is absent

I draw closer to him with the memory of him

The smell of him, the freshness of his scent

His essence remains

He is my man

The pain, frustration, and battles he faces

The courage it would take

My Black man maneuvering through life

Come home to your wife

Our marriage bed is ready

Sleep will escape

and pleasures will be found

Her Name is Grace

I need to kiss away your problems, aggravations, and worries

Desirous of holding you

pouring my love upon your flesh

Tantalizing your manliness

I shift your thought processes

ease your stress

You deserve the best

of me

All that I have to give

You deserve my respect, compassion, understanding, and care

Love, reciprocated

He is my Man

CHAPTER 5

Nubile Love

My husband regarded my inexperience and timidity with forbearance and amused indulgence as he instructed me on the rudiments of lovemaking. This reciprocated foreplay catapulted me on a journey of discovery. The fluidness of his skill unraveled and removed many barriers, enabling me to learn and explore his depths. Nubile love unshackled our coming together as husband and wife. Our union was explosive, uninhibited, and carefree. Joy penetrated my very soul as every inch of my body came alive. I transitioned into nubile love.

I have bloomed into a woman full-grown, and full of nectar. Aged like a fine wine nestled within the confines of its amphorae, I no longer waited for my time. My sensualness was at its peak as I awaited the kiss of my Black man. I tarried for the moment, uncorked, and awakened by the intoxicating smell of him. As I bloomed, I began allowing him to handle me with care. He lifted the crystal glass to his lips and inhaled the aromatic fragrance of my flower. He relished the strength of my juice and became enthralled with my sherry.

I am nubile and have awakened to my sexuality.

I have allowed my love to mature and grow in the intimacy of understanding who I am as a woman. No longer am I afraid to allow him to sheath himself within me. I allow my voice to be heard and steer him to the freshness that I present. Allowing him to unleash potent pleasures that have been asleep.

My Black man shall not defile me,

For whoso findeth, a wife findeth a good thing, and obtaineth favour of the Lord. Proverbs 18:22

And because he has found me,

[Our] marriage is honourable in all, and the bed undefiled... Hebrews 13:11

I have loosed the woman in me, the erotic desires that caused me to quiver in fear and shame are now bold and intrepid in my marriage bed. Expressing my desires, needs, and wants, I cleverly yet timidly give in to his entreaty, allowing those explored nuances of love to awaken.

I have become the ripe flower, ready for the harvest.

Patricia Johnson

Fearfully and Wonderfully Made

He presents his maleness before me in all its glory

The splendor of him

The baldness of his head glistened with droplets from the sea

Self-assured in what he possesses

He walks across the white sands into the stillness of the night

I can hear the waves against the shores

But nothing could stop the fluidness of his gait

Puissant

Steady

Confident

No shame or arrogance

just understanding who he is

Assured that no imposters are within

I cannot hold back my smile

My shame is gone

I stand before him with the moon at my back

The excitement of watching him as he moves in the night

Becoming part of the landscape, no beginning or end

He stands before me

No movement

I feel his breath, the heat of him

Her Name is Grace

He is lost within the darkness

And then

His majesty pierces my reality as the moon casts its glow

The dampness upon his skin

The touch of his hand gently holding mine

The gentle smile that plays across his face

His look intense

My heart began to race

I in my glory

Unashamed

Self-confident

Assured

His eyes taste of me

Devouring me

Loving me

The intensity of his glare

No judgment or condemnation

He sees me as I am

Not through the lens of me

Or how I view myself

This pouring of love caused me to cry

I could not understand how

this beautiful, tall, strong, black man could love me

Love me in my insecurities, and feelings of less than

Patricia Johnson

This man, my man

my husband

Views me with eyes that behold a beauty

It far exceeds me

He sees me through the eyes of God

And through his love

I see His love

I am

fearfully and wonderfully made!

Your Vineyard

Walk through the vineyard,

stop and take a sip

My wine

My sweets

will give you pleasure

Tantalize your senses

And hold you forever

Take this cup, my love

It is filled with drink

Your thirst shall be quenched

Walk amongst the roses

and peel the petals back

Expose my bud

and you may sup upon that

Take your fill of me

Take me at will

Your dainties await

Desires shall grow

Your strength shall rise

Patricia Johnson

Pull back the tender pedals between my thighs

It is all for you, my love

I am ready for the harvest

Walk through my vineyard and take a sip

You shall become drunken

from the strength of me

Stumbling and unsteady on your feet

Indulge

Imbibe

Become intoxicated

Because you love me

Her Name is Grace

I Am Yours

My garden sits upon the rise of my flesh

The flatness of my belly

will attest

The smoothness of my skin

reacts to your touch

A love unfathomable

And I cannot contain it

The joy that I feel when I reach that part of you

My needs ease as I move beneath you

It is like heaven my love

A love like this

Can never repeat

My treasure

My chest

My skin

Afire with the taste of you

Patricia Johnson

The Maleness of You

The maleness of you

The strength of your hands glide across my breasts

Only for you my pleasure center responds

Those hands gentle but strong

They assault my body on this, a journey of love

You are my love, my heart, the rhythm that beats within

You are my star and my moon

You captured me

Only you cause a reaction

And only to your male attraction

This man

My man

My husband

He who enfolds me with himself

I am beneath the strength of you

Receiving you

We are one, moving to a song of love specific to us

You have penetrated me, pinned me

Happily,

I am no longer free

You have taken me to that spot

Her Name is Grace

Yes, that one

G…

It is glorious with you

You are part of me

Breathing with me

Carrying me

Leading me

How splendid is our dance

Is this real or am I dreaming?

This wondrous ride from the heat of you

The sweat of your brow

The movement of your hips as you bring me closer

Your hands at the base of my back

Your fingertips pressed into my spine

My mind floating in time

My senses filled to capacity

I hold you, touch you, lose myself with you

I scream out,

I scratch you

but I don't mean to

My hands are gentle yet strong

Clasping your sides as I move you along

I close my eyes and release a deep sigh

Through tears

Patricia Johnson

The tenderness you possess

Your handling of me,

Fulfillment, joy, and the wonderment of our love

You moved with me, guided me, and your spirit through me

The mysteries of a love so true

One that God gave to me and you

One captured only from above

God's gift to us

Husband and Wife

I am Yours

Yours!

Her Name is Grace

The Water is Ready

I stand and watch from my window

The sun is high up on the horizon

The breeze is slight as the curtains move

The heat of the day

causing me to sway

My brow is moist, and my throat is parched

A cool drink of you

I must…

Squinting my eyes to adjust my view

Baby I cannot wait to see you

The day seems long

I am lonely for you

My Prince, I need you

My temperature rises

as I catch sight of you

Walking across the fresh-cut grass

through the opening in the trees

Your keys in hand and rucksack on your back

The railroaders trade heavily upon you

Your cap a little twisted

Your shirt a mess

Unbuttoned to expose your chest

It appears you are soaked through

The hard day's work beating you

I know what to do

I greet you at the door with a smile and a kiss

Removing the rucksack from your shoulder

the keys from your hand

your hat from your head

I draw you a bath

Add some bubbles the way you like

Undress you

Caress you

And yes

Gently bathe you

Guiding you to our suite of delights

I lay you upon our bed

your head on the pillow

I massage you

The front

then the back

My hands moving down your spine

Releasing the tension and stress of the day

I am unable to touch you

and remain unmoved

by the beauty of you

I begin to stir

I taste you

I take a sip from your cup

until it runneth over

The pleasure of you

I need you

Your water is ready

Patricia Johnson

A Good Thing

I lay upon our marriage bed

I am waiting with anticipation

My husband is on the way

His love I have always known

This intimacy is new

I hear his footsteps across the floor

My heart leaps with excitement

I do not know what to expect

He is my first

My love

My heart

I promised my Father

That I would wait and be a good thing

I would wait on his promise

to allow a man to find a wife

This man has found me

A wife of his own

His good thing

His build is of Adonis

His walk is as smooth as a panther's stealth in the night

His ebony skin glowing from within

Her Name is Grace

I cannot wait

He is mine tonight

I lay upon our marriage bed

It is pure and undefiled

He approaches

I am anxious

I am giddy

I am ready

He touches my lips tenderly

Placing a finger beneath my chin he kisses me on the cheek

He slowly ever so gently removes my negligee

His eyes travel the length of me

Without a sound, he continues to peruse me

I lay a quiver

Shaking from head to toe

Unfamiliar and unsure

I could not move

His gaze lingers at the v of my thighs

Tossing my gown to the floor he lay on the bed

No shirt, slacks, or shoes

His nakedness

A robe of glory

He looks at me

A sheepish grin that only I knew

Patricia Johnson

His power

His strength

His Blackness

bold

as is his beauty

Mystifying

A night to remember

His fingers play with my hair

as he searches the depths of me

His eyes roam over what belongs to him

Him alone!

I am feeling flustered

a blush begins to rise

He continues his assault on my body while penetrating my mind

And asks me the question, "May I make love to you?"

I am taken aback

for I am his wife

I do not understand the question

And he asks me again

"May I make love to you?"

Too shy to look his way

I turn my head to look away

with a gentle finger, he turns my face

back to his

Her Name is Grace

His breath warm upon my cheek

Staring intently

His cognac-colored eyes

A third time he asks

"May I make love to you?"

I slowly, tentatively part my lips

As I respond my voice begins to shake

"Why do you need to ask, I am your wife?"

His smile widens into a deep grin

The whiteness of his teeth against the darkness of his flesh

Oh, my

Dear God, he is a magnificent specimen

Gently he caresses my face and held my stare

He says,

"You are my wife. Yes."

with a gentle nod of his head

"You are a woman first

Your voice should be heard

I dare not presume you are ready for this

Out of love and respect for your feelings

the timidity in you

I ask, may I make love to you?

My woman

My wife!"

I finally understood why God allowed me to be found

God thank you for this night

This man

This specific man

This son

His love was profound

My feelings and concerns were first upon his mind

Not the pleasures he would find

This moment

One I shall never forget

True love is selfless and not pushed by lust

This man genuinely loves

me

And in you my Father I will continue to trust

I am a good thing

Marriage Bed

I roll with you

I stroll with you

I open my heart to you

I swing my hips within your sight

I turn my head and tilt it to the light

My stature is sure

My smooth brown skin

The color of coffee with a hint of cream mixed in

The journey of love and intoxication

Leaves me high

Delirious from your kisses

On the peak of this mountain

The sun is rising high

The brightness of this moment

Tasting of my breasts

I spiral into blissful happiness

Your calloused hands

Marking paths across my body

My stomach, hips, and thighs

My legs, calves, and toes

I hunger and thirst for you

Patricia Johnson

I cannot hold out much longer

But I do not wish this to end

The feel of you

The touch of your hands, and chest upon me

The flavor of you

I need you

I want you

My heart is racing, screaming, coming alive

The moaning from you

Pleads with me

Excites me yet more

I am throbbing with passion

I must release it

I am enraptured with your offer

My body about to falter

You can my love

Touch me there

The essence of me

Love resounds

An echo once more

It is all because of you.

You are the one

My espoused

My man

Her Name is Grace

My husband

No longer two

This night we are one

Body

Soul

Spirit

I am locked with you

A dance of two

Yet we are one flesh

We are upon our marriage bed

All is good

Complete me my darling

Patricia Johnson

My Knight in Shining Armor

I lay beside you

My knight in shining armor

Defender

Protector

Liberator

I open the fragileness of my flower to allow you entrance

I expose the rosebud of my pleasure that the gateway would be sure

I am no tease but want to please

And this–

The sweet taste of my honey

I give

My rosebud

My pleasure point

only for your touch

Your body is robust and permeates my scent

It is you my knight that I desire

Tis you that set my body afire

My knight in shining armor

I expose the center of my goodness

For your lips to drink

Her Name is Grace

From the planted vine of my body that you seek

I adore you

The smell of you

The touch of you

The, yes that part of you

My knight in shining armor my love for you awaits

My blessed jewels

I have cared for them for so long

Tending to my garden until the season was ripe

No one could enter

Only you my knight

Harvest me, my knight

Tend to your garden

My hesitation

Unsteady, please

My murmurs make me fall to my knees

My knight

My knight in shining armor

I awakened to you this day

I spread myself to please myself with you

I allow you entrance

But–

Will you

Will you my knight

Patricia Johnson

Touch the fruits I present

Will you free me

from this pain that lies within the need

Will you fill me with your joy

The erotic pleasure that rises

Take me in the storm

The roaring of the seas

My heart throbbing

I cannot breathe

Lull my cries

My petitions

My supplications to you

Have your way in the garden

I beg you

Kissed by the Son

I arose early in the morning to the sun warming my face

I reached across and touched the hand of my black man

He turned his head and looked at me

A soft smile lit his features

The dark brown of him mesmerized my soul

The force of him caused my body to shake

The love in him allowed my tears to flow

My man has been kissed by the Son

He protects me with himself

He loves me

Infinitely

I rolled to the left and placed my face on his chest

I pressed my leg between his and felt the muscles therein

I stroked him, he caressed me

Holding me with his eyes

excites me

My man has been kissed by the Son

He protects me with himself

He loves me

Infinitely

Patricia Johnson

The sun rose higher

The heat

Not from the sun

But the passion of my flower

awakened

I love this man

My soul cried for him

And as the sun rose

He pulled me closer till I am prostrate upon him

His hardness, the firmness, no fat about him

The masculinity exuded by this man

Compassion

Tenderness

The ability to love

This man, kissed by the Son

My man has been kissed by the Son

He protects me with himself

He loves me

Infinitely

The only man

I have eyes for no other

He squeezed me

Kissed the tip of my nose

Her Name is Grace

I wanted more of him

I needed the feel of him

But—

Work he must

My man has been kissed by the Son

He protects me with himself

He loves me

Infinitely

My man, providing for his family

The horn of the engine calls

Woo, Woo

It was time to go

Laying me to the side he rose, standing before me

I had to shield my eyes from the brightness of his glory

But I watched him

His nakedness before me

I allow my eyes to roam

His toes and feet

Ankles and calves

His thighs and yes, his manliness

The flatness of his abdomen

I continued to roam

His chest is massive

Patricia Johnson

Muscles rippling all about

His stretched-out arms had the wingspan of an eagle

His strong neck holding that magnificent head

Laughing eyes and a smile so genuine

I am flushed and turning red

My man has been kissed by the Son

He protects me with himself

He loves me

Infinitely

My temperature rising and not because of the sun

This impressively beautiful man stood before me

Verily–

Loves me

His face, body, mind, and soul

My muse

I stretched forth my hand and touch his

He looked at me longingly

Lifting my hand to his lips

Nibbling upon them, causing my toes to curl

Again, tears begin to fall

This man

My man

Kissed by the Son

Her Name is Grace

I am so blessed to have him

I never imagined a love like this

My man has been kissed by the Son

He protects me with himself

He loves me

Infinitely

A word

A touch

A gentle kiss

Through His love

he inspired me to be my best self

He encouraged me to excel and not be afraid of new things

He exposed me to a love I have never known

My man has been kissed by the Son

Patricia Johnson

My Man

I search you

I allow my heart to pierce you

I watch you

I hear you

I make love to you

Without touching you

My body greeted him

with a rapturous response

I tremble for the want of him

Loving to watch him

I am so in love

Attentive

Referencing

Adoring

Devoted

To this man of mine kissed by the Son

Lowering himself to reach me

Upon our marriage bed

I begin to salivate at the thought of his love

Her Name is Grace

Hoping

Desiring

Pleading with my body

He smiled

Reading my thoughts

He knows me so well

But

He kissed me on my forehead and shook his head

no

Work he must

my love

"I will return with all that you desire…"

He says

I love you Patricia

My love is only for you

Your beauty and charms I look for at the breaking of each dawn

You, my love, are the woman I chose

You are perfect for me

You are loyal

Lovely

And true

You are my muse

You encourage me

Uplift me

Patricia Johnson

Hold me

Never do you talk down to me

Criticize or treat me like a boy

You my love are a precious gem

I waited for you

Got to know you

Fell in love with you

Married you

Patricia

And with his words

I am kissed by the Son

CHAPTER 6

Progeny Love Is a Love That Produces a Descendant or Offspring

It is written, "…God blessed them and God said unto them, be fruitful, and multiply, and replenish the earth, and subdue it…"Genesis 1:28. And it was this belief that pushed our love to another level, "…children are a heritage of the Lord: and the fruit of the womb is his reward," Psalm 127:3. Our love transcended to a degree that wanted and needed to express the love of God by bringing forth our offspring.

This love is another means to augment that glorious union of the two becoming one flesh. "Thus saith the Lord, the redeemer, and he that formed thee from the womb, I am the Lord that maketh all things," Isaiah 44:24.

This coming together is more than the pleasure, the magical moments, the tenderness, and the drawing one from another. This union is a bond that shrouds a husband and wife within the veil of holy matrimony. This bond is not just the physical but also the spiritual fusion before God which creates a heritage of the Lord.

Patricia Johnson

Woman

I carried you

Inside of me

Asleep

Taken from

My rib

My womb

Created

Woman

I was not to be alone

Cleave unto my wife

My woman

The seed of me

Spread inside of you

My posterity

My woman

Your field

Seeds planted

Living waters

Her Name is Grace

The Son

Ripe

Water flows

From you

My woman

The fruit

You bear

Brought forth

In His season

My children

My offspring

My heritage

My progeny

My woman

Patricia Johnson

Creation

I am encapsulated within the coiled seminiferous tubules. I am nestled lovingly in the confines of my testes and as I begin to awaken to the touch and smell of you, I can no longer control the journey that has begun to stir.

I have dreamed of pouring myself into your warmth, into your essence. This odyssey of love takes me on the shores of the epididymis. I grow with vigor and strength and the softness of your touch, the anticipation that rises, the yearning of your cries, and the intense aura of you create helplessness within. The slightest movement of your hands, the heat of your breath, and the taste of your lips captivate me.

I am determined to fill you, to become one with you.

I am swiftly moving, swimming excitedly through the vas deferens, a space that propels me with a quick smoothness as I begin to dance a dance of love.

I stay my course and I land at the ampulla, waiting for this roller coaster ride to continue. But, lo and behold, the waterfall of secretions pours upon me from the vesicle. Still, I press on. Impatiently, I jump for joy as I ride through the seminal vesicle. Oh! My darling, my sweet, I am bathed in the intoxicating sea of love. Hold on to me! Continue your assault of love. I need the heat of you. Your scent, your eyes, and your sweat are causing a rise that I cannot contain. Your passion supports me, strengthening me. Your moves, the sway, and the thrust of your hips encourage me.

The gentle touch of your lips pushing me draws me, guiding me through the ejaculatory ducts toward the end of my ride. I can see the light on the horizon while gliding through the prostate gland of milky fluid. I bask in its plentifulness. I begin to grow in its power, its potency.

I am almost there, my love.

Our oneness is all I feel, all I need. I'm pushing, hurrying for your delights. I have passed through the far end of the valley of the urethra and the explosiveness of my journey has brought me to a new dimension within the heat of your love. I have erupted like a volcano into you, amalgamating a union that has taken me on a wild ride bursting into multi-colored rainbows.

This love, this power of creation has spent me, yet again!

Patricia Johnson

Dance of Night

Out of the dance of the night

I find myself full of you

Your sons, your daughters

Your posterity

grows within me

I feel the fullness of you

Your sons, your daughters

Nestled in my womb

They grow and move within

I think of the blessings that soon will extend

Your sons, your daughters

From your loins to mine

God's most precious gift throughout time

My body swells with the love of you

The joy of life as we have never known

Labor

Travail

God blessed me in that

Soon my love

Her Name is Grace

Your posterity presents

His head, her head

Ready to arrive

as I push these blessings from inside

I push

I bear down with all that I've got!

Crying from a mixture of joy and pain

I look up at you

holding my hand in the power of you

Your eyes manifest compassion

joy

hope

Your posterity

Ready to come forth

Penetrating

Pain

Heat

Fire

Explosive

Water

Cooling

Joy

No pain

We rejoice

The laughter in your eyes
Caught me by surprise
The joy upon your face
Uncertainty erased

Tears
the thumping of your heart
the tilt of your head
the tenderness in your touch
volumes are spoken

I hear
I see
I feel
I love

Your sons, your daughters
shall grow in the strength of you
The love of you
The character of you
The influence of you
The giving of you

Your posterity

shall carry you!

Patricia Johnson

Progeny

My children are growing

Becoming

Men and women in time

This road is hard

What will they find?

Too often they will hear

Black men are runners

afraid to be fathers

They do not care or want to be bothered

Black men are in prison

Nonsupport on their mind

You are not worth it

No one cares about you

You will never make it

Education is a waste

Sell a dime and you will be fine

The system is against you

Death is knocking at your door

There's only one thing you are good for

Pull the trigger

Her Name is Grace

Nigger!

My children, offspring, my progeny

I need an ear

Hear me and do not fear

I am a Black man

I am your father

You will never have to fear

I am near

I am here to raise you

Nurture and teach you

Protect

Love

And educate you

I am here to guide you

Enlighten you through

Prayer

Righteousness

Relationship

Holy Spirit

Jesus

Abba

Father

Patricia Johnson

Counselor

Confidant

Friend

I will teach you to lean on God

Feed from his Word

I will show you what it means

for your voice to be heard

My children, my offspring, my progeny

You mean so much to me

A love like this no other compare

I will not deliberately hurt you,

but I will chastise you

I will never debase, humiliate, or belittle you,

But I will correct you

You are my seed

God's gift to me

I must be precise with your care and guidance

confirming who you are

Prepare you

Never leave you

Her Name is Grace

Life can be cruel and sometimes hard

I will be near to help you along

You are worth my time, energy, my life

all that I have

My children, my offspring, my progeny

You mean so much to me

I love you!

Patricia Johnson

Beautiful Black Babies

My beautiful Black babies

as dark as the night

you are so precious

but there will be a fight

melanin-filled

light, honey, cocoa, and cream

chocolate, dark

a hue of blue

your melanin

does not

define you

they will call you names

make you feel shame

make you cry

cast you in the shadows

of a never-ending lie

they will make you think

Black is bad

your voice is small

minuscule

Her Name is Grace

insignificant

powerless at best

My beautiful Black babies

oppressed in your nakedness

magazines, tv, ads, programs, and plays

the stage, behind the scenes, and all those things

attacks will certainly come

don't try to defend

My beautiful Black babies

melanin-filled

light, honey, cocoa, and cream

chocolate, dark

a hue of blue

your melanin does not define you

Strong

Lineage

Kings

Queens

Leaders

Risen

Stand

on their shoulders

Straight

Tall

Confident

A force to behold

Not a victim

Or miscalculation

Less than

Or fake

You are

A treasure

A chest of wonder

God makes

no mistakes

Children

My darling children

God's gift

Listen

Open your ears and hear what I have to say

I am a man

Not a white man's boy

I am strong

I work hard to meet your needs

I am no beggar

Slothful or afraid to care for you

Pray for you

Play with you or

Bathe you

America the land of the free!

Liberty

Educate

Procreate

Work

Live

Communities'

Cities and

Towns

Why are we followed around?

Our demise is always on their mind

Imminent

Rogue

Thug

Heartless

Cruel

Bad

Color

Black

Who knew?

America!

How could this be?

Fear

Angst

Hostility

Depression

Self-pity

Shame

Her Name is Grace

Inadequacy

Placed on our back

Mental

Emotions

Feelings

Attacks

Struggling to stay on track

Justice!

Call on her

Shake her

Wake her

Outrage her

Make her work for you

Making laws

Changing laws

Courts on high

My children

Firm

Sure

True

Patricia Johnson

Steadfast

Listen

Speak

Voices

What more can you do?

Baby Boy

I watch my baby boy

His fine black skin

Kissed by God

Born into sin

A world that treats him badly

Tells him he's nothing

Just like his daddy

I watch my baby boy

I am awash with pain

The agony of his growing

in a world so untamed

Torn to pieces

by the power of the tongue

Life and death

Words

Live or die

Love, joy, and peace

Hate, sadness, and grief

I watch my baby boy

Patricia Johnson

His fine black skin

Kissed by God

Born into sin

A world that treats him badly

Tells him he's nothing

Just like his daddy

I watch my baby boy

Crawl

Toddle

Stumble

And fall

Learning to stand

Walking without my hand

Independent

Confident

Sure

Moving about

He wants to get out

My tears I capture

in the palm of my hands

Her Name is Grace

Unsteady

Dependent

Doubting

Uncertainty

Knowing what he faces tempts me

Reflection of me

Mother

Teacher

Counselor

Confidant

Example

Did I?

Could I?

Should I?

I let go!

I step back!

I watch this man

standing before me

Standing tall, steadfast

on his own

Patricia Johnson

I am no longer his anchor

Just a piece of his puzzle

Securely tied to Christ

he walks ahead

Between the church pews

Amongst the onlookers and oohs

At the alter

On his knees

Before Christ and our Father above

He begins to pray and extends his hand

Calling on God for the forgiveness of his sins

I watch my baby boy who is now a man

Intertwine himself in the Master's hand

The blood of Jesus has washed him clean

No blotches, sin, transgressions, or pain

Now washed in the blood of He who reigns

My baby boy, my son

this young man of mine

Chose to stand for someone

and freely give his life

Not to me or his dad but to his

Father!

CHAPTER 7

Profound Love Is That Which Is Very Great, Intense, or Deeply Knowing.

Jesus wept, John 11:35-36…behold how he loved him!

S ome have stated that men should not cry and if they do, it is a sign of weakness that should never be displayed, but Jesus did!

This rhetoric spread throughout centuries, yet the strongest man, the purest man, the Lamb of God, wept. The power of God's love is great and when He loves, it never fails us. His love strengthens us, encourages us, and shows us the way to pure love through him. It cannot be matched by mankind. However, there are times in our lives when our love is so profound, so intense that we weep, as did Christ.

Women are emotional beings, and we often use our tears to measure joy, pain, hurt, suffering, or sorrow. But our men, Black men, can also be brought to tears. This is especially true of a man that understands, just like Jesus understood, that to weep is not a lack of masculinity. It exposes the humanness, compassion, and empathy that lives within their strength.

There are times within a marriage when weeping will find its way, cascading from the heart of a man before his woman, his wife. I was amazed to espy my husband's weeping come forth in a torrent that could not be quenched when he cared for me, prayed for me, or petitioned God for me.

I feel deeply saddened that we fall into the game of what is or is not masculine. We should not stigmatize or belittle our men and cause them to feel shame for engaging an emotion that is a part of the very fabric of their manhood. Weeping does not diminish or detract from their manhood. It exposes a vulnerable and loving heart, sensitivity, truth about self, and freedom without judgment. It demands courage and the knowledge of who you are as a man.

A husband is the head and covering for his wife and his prayer holds power. The potency of which can cause a man to fall to his knees and cry out to God. Words are spoken from his heart as the floodgates of his tears fall freely from him. God sees our tears, and He does respond, not always with a yes, but He answers. Remove the disdain and shame that we attach to our sons as they become infected by our view of manhood, and teach them that men do cry because Jesus wept!

My Black man Wept

Jesus Wept

My Black man wept

He wept for me

He wept over me

He wept with me

My Black man's pain

Did not turn into shame

The tears fell

Running freely before me

My Black man wept

His love was not diminished

His heart was open

The flood came

A torrential rain

He cried

The sadness he could not hide

Incredulity upon his face

Shedding tears was not a disgrace

Flowing freely from his heart

A place of hidden shadows in the dark

He understood

To cry is to be free

He opened his heart

He could finally see
The perils of holding on
The hate, pain, and being a pawn

Exposure

Disquietude

Agitation

Panic

Alarm

The ridicule and fear of labels on your back
Sissified

Wimpish

Effeminate and soft
My Black man understood all that

And,

He wept!
Jesus wept

Can I Submit?

I am your woman, and I would love to be submissive to you

my husband

My prior hurts, pains, and love abuse causes me much shame

I want to follow you

Godly man that you are

But how can I trust that your love will not hurt my heart

I want to believe that you will lead me

on a path of righteousness

I want to believe that your love is real

and not led by lust

I want to believe that all you say is true

How can I be assured that you won't cause me pain

How will I know that you will not cause me shame

I want to follow you and submit to your hand

But how can I

if you are a controlling man

I need to know

How can I be sure you will love me

and not change me

I have been there and done that

That pain has not gone

I have not been released from the debasement he caused

How can I trust that the pain and shame of it all

Patricia Johnson

will not carry on…
With You

His Response

I am a man that loves you

I am a man that honors the vows he made to you

I am a man that is affirmed by our God

Nurtured, tutored, and learned by Him

He created me

Molded me

And His word showed me

My darling, I do not take lightly the commitment that I made

I stood before you and our Father

and declared my love for you

I am to love you as Christ so loved the church

Not shame you

Belittle or debase you

I love you

The whole you

Any broken part of you

I allowed God's word to transform me

lead and guide me

so that I may nurture you

lead and guide you

properly

I am not your past hurt and pain

You must lay it to rest

Patricia Johnson

I am a man of my word

My love is concrete

My love is sure

My Father has chosen me to pour his love upon you

and pour it I shall

until it overflows

Then you will know

that my love is real

Not manipulative

Arrogant

Boastful

Selfish or demanding

My love is strong

Resilient

Accepting

Long-suffering

Gentle

Kind

Patient

And most of all

It's God's love

for you

My Lovely Hard Worker, Mother, And Wife

I got off early from work

I was tired but knew I had to cook, clean,

and help with homework

The children would be coming home from school

and my husband wanted his food

I am exhausted, toiling at my day job to help ends meet

I get into my ride hoping traffic would subside

The sooner I get started the sooner I will have

a moment to myself

Traffic is light and I am home in ten

I want to let my hair down and relax in some bubbles

without a care

The peace, quiet, and solitude are what I need

Just a moment, please

I pull into the driveway, my man's truck was there

Oh well,

Today is not the day for peace and quiet

or time to pray

I opened the door to enter our home

Threw my coat to the floor

In amazement, under my feet,

Patricia Johnson

bright red rose petals

Everywhere I turned I could see

smell

aromatic petals

Slowly I walked through the house

My man and children, I could not find

I took a step back and refocused

Standing at the bottom of the stairs

to our bedroom

A new fragrance mingling with those roses

Frankincense and myrrh

stirring my senses

My ears began to tingle at the melodies of time past

Hey, that's Teddy Pendergrass

I followed the trail up the stairs

and into the warmth of my bedroom

with delicate care placed across the bed

a robe,

gown,

towel,

and a note addressed to me

My lovely, hard worker, mother, and wife

Today the children and I decided you needed a break; your bubbles are waiting, your candles are lit, and your wine has been chilled and poured into your glass.

I notice all that you do, the strength of you, the caring in you, the LOVE...
You deserve so much more.
Today is your day.
You will not be disturbed, not a chore, or hear me snore.
The lights are turned down, covers are pulled back.
The sheets are warmed and you will not lack.
I plumped your pillows and will leave for the night.
This is beyond sexual intimacy but showing you that...

WE LOVE YOU!

We do not take for granted the things that you do, sometimes we forget to show you.

My lovely, hard worker, mother, and wife - thank you and goodnight.

— Your loving family

Patricia Johnson

Love Reciprocated

My man received shocking news at work

The boss called him into his office

This was not a joke

They laid him off

Said things were slow

They could not use him, and they had to let him go

He walked to his office

Despair

Defeated

Feeling alone

Not wanting to go home

He did not want to tell his wife

Would she understand?

Grabbing the box, they left in his office

he filled it with his things

Security at the door

to escort him off the floor

He looked around once more

25 years

How do I face my woman, my wife

How do I tell her I can no longer provide

The job is gone

This is all I have ever done

Her Name is Grace

I never missed a day, never late
Always attentive
Turning things in on time
The job came first, and my life was usually there
And now I find myself being escorted from the office
the department I started
I do not understand,
and I did not see it coming
How do I face my woman, my wife, the love of my life
How do I tell her that my job was terminated
ended
gone
I ponder these thoughts and realize that the sum of me
at this place, lay in a cardboard box
I am now free
I cannot see
beyond the here and now
I have no plan
What next

I do not know what to say to her
She is accustomed to my indulging
caring, pampering, providing, and dating her
Where do I get the words to pour out of my heart
and explain my circumstance?
What will I find
Anger and hostility directed at my back

Patricia Johnson

Yells and screams at my lack

No job nigga, that's what they say

A black woman on the attack

because I have no pay

Is the rhetoric right

I must pray

I pull into my driveway

A two-door garage, her Mercedes Benz in one

and my GMC in the other

Affluent,

but now that has changed

I have no job to keep her, entertain her, or bedazzle her

I no longer have the financial means to continue this life

How can I tell my wife

This is not going to be easy to say, I know I will lose her

I am a black man pushed out the door

Nonetheless, I walk to the porch

and there she stood

Always waiting for her man

I move in close and look intently into her eyes

I tell her the news and brace myself

for what is sure to come

But what she gave me

I am perplexed…

She hugged me, squeezed me,

and gave me a kiss

Her Name is Grace

She investigated my face with a smile of compassion

Hugging me again she stood on her toes

and kissed my nose

My dear man, my darling Black man

My husband, my life

Although you worked outside of our home

you trusted me with the funds you owned

I took those monies, my darling Black man,

and over the years invested,

worked it and it grew

And as it did, I began to work too

Consulting others and telling them what to do

You have a Proverbs 31 wife

Sitting idle, slothful, doing nothing to build for you

That is not me, my love

I rise early to prepare your meals

and make sure your needs are met

In and out of bed

I love you

We professed it to each other

I know you love me

You have always shown me

You exposed your heart to me

You have always provided

Excellent

Undisturbed

Your love for me surpassed

Patricia Johnson

all that I have known
You must see
it is reciprocated by me
I have your back, I had it all along
You are not a nigger, slothful, or in lack
My love is unconditional, adhesive, concrete
It is not weak, superficial, or pretend
My love for you is not a game of hurt and pain
I am a woman of my word
I do not yell or curse at you
Belittle you or mock you
You are my man and I love you
I am a Proverb 31 wife
I gotcha back
Welcome home
we will not lack
I handled your business with flair and style
We did well
God blessed us and we need not a thing
Our house is paid off
the cars too
We give to the church without missing a beat
Prospered by God's grace
I am a Proverb 31 woman
I will take care of you
Indulge, bathe,
and date you

Her Name is Grace

My love, my man, husband, and spouse

My black man

I love you

it's reciprocated

Patricia Johnson

The S Word

He knows me

My Black man adores me

He doesn't idolize me

He understands that our relationship is not just

sexual intimacy

But love at its highest

He knows my likes and dislikes

He knows me

He knows what hides behind my smile

The gentle touch of a hand

The way I flirt with him

He understands

He knows what I am feeling

Whether I am down

or on high

He knows the smell of me

The touch of me

Every inch of me

My Black man is no ordinary man

I will follow him

Her Name is Grace

Not question him

Why

You may not understand

But I will give it to you straight

My Black man

A man who loves the Lord

He is strong in faith

Never interprets scripture to suit his needs

He allows the word to conform him to the image of

Christ and that is what I need

He doesn't walk one way

expecting me to walk another

He is in tune with me

My submission to him

I give to no other

He has proven himself to be

A man after God's heart

The apple of his eye

And one who will not part

My black man will not stray

from God's word

He will not manipulate me

Or beat me with the **S** word

Submission is a choice

One I freely give

Patricia Johnson

First to my Father, Jesus, and Holy Spirit
Then to him
My man
My Black man
My husband

Submission taunted me
Oppressed me
Brutalized
And beat me
Don't say the **S** word
It will offend
I will not release my autonomy
My freedom
My life
Submission is like throwing the dice

But God…

Showed me, taught me, loved on me
Through you,
My Black man
My husband

That the **S** word was not to offend
Oppress
Brutalize

Her Name is Grace

Or beat me down

Submission is a release and the willingness to let self-go

And place your heart, your love, and your life in the hands of your spouse

It was hard but God showed me what to do

He gave me to a man that loved me

Like you…

My Black man never throws submission or subjection in my face

he loves me

guides me and teaches the word to me

Bible study for him and me

A way of life

A purpose

A path to righteousness and love so true

One that is whole, concrete, and complete

The **S** word

Don't let it hold you

Bind you

Cripple you

Allow the **S** word to free you

Subjection or submission you choose

Don't be afraid to say it, learn it, and live it

The **S** word

Let it come through

Patricia Johnson

SUBMISSION or SUBJECTION

Which one are you

Her Name is Grace

Caregiver

My bathwater is ready

The bubbles cascading down the side of the tub

It is in overflow

The perfumed smell of lilac

The room is soft

aglow with candles

my man, my Black man

he lifts me

kisses me

gently centers me in the tub

he knows my likes dislikes

and those things that make me comfortable

my favorite bath pillow

placed behind my head

the water is warm the aroma sweet

it is relaxing and causing me to sleep

no, my love

no sleeping in the tub

lean forward a little and let me scrub your back

relax my darling

I will handle you with care

you are my charge, and I would not dare

abuse, hurt or misuse you

gently I will touch the folds of you

the length of you

the woman of you

I will clean you from head to toe

I will massage you caress you

and speak kind soft words to you

I will not manipulate you

it is about me caring for you

showing you a new depth of my love for you

your comfort your care

and washing your hair

I will suds it

condition it

and comb your curls

you do not have to ask or prompt my love

I know what you need before the words are spoken

relax

this time is for you

relax and feel the warmth of the water

relax and allow me to pamper you

allow your senses to rejoice

in the pleasure of you

pleasures that will refresh you

and make you feel new

my darling lady

my charge

I love you

Her Response

my dearest Black man, your love for me always shines

my thoughts of you are full of happiness and contentment divine
you are a wonder I have told you before

my Black man

the man that I adore

your love for me is so much more

than the act of sexual intimacy

in my illness you love me

respect me

and tenderly care for me

in my illness, you provide

all that I need

you stimulate my mind with such kind deeds

you walk with me

talk with me and read to me as well

you my darling Black man I cannot dispel

words I do not have to express the magnitude of

how grateful I am to you

your love has caused me to lose my mind

and no other man will ever find

what you possess for me

the person that you are in totality

you have it all

Black man of God

you pray for me, lay with me, feed me and bathe me

it is a hard job, but you make it flawless

thank you, my darling man

thank you for all that I am

it is because God granted my petition

and blessed me with you.

I do not cry

it is because of you

I do not lose hope

I no longer want to die

I am not alone

fasting and praying me through

That is what you do

night and day

day and night

when you think I do not hear

you must know all that you give

all that you do

all that you say

all of you

from the center of my heart and the depths of my soul,

I say thank you

to my God-fearing man

I Love You Like Christ So Loved The Church

My man lay beside me and pulled me close

he held me, kissed me, and then let me go

he wanted nothing of me

just to say goodnight

He rose from his side of the bed and walked

slowly to the closet

as he opened the door,

he looked back at me

and this is all he spoke

PRAY

he gently closed the door

I could hear as he fell to the floor

prostrate

he began calling out to our mighty God

I could hear him calling the name of Jesus

I could hear him calling Holy Spirit

All is still

As I lay listening to the quiet of the night

my eyes wide peeking into the darkness

I could still hear a faint cry

Pleadings

Requests

Petitions

My man was praying for me

I could not help but hear what he cried,

He was so passionate,

so fervent and sure

It blew my mind

I have never heard a man praying for me

Let alone with such ferocity

This one was praying for me

me

hearing him cry out

pleading the blood of Jesus over my life

a cascade of tears began to fall upon my pillow

a pouring so torrential the deluge would not end

I could not comprehend the immensity of his love

The gravity

The weight of this thing called **LOVE**

My mind reels

The revelation of his care and commitment to me

to us, to our marriage, and the vows we spoke

This man

My man

My Black man

On his face in that private space

at the foot of the cross

Petitioning God our Father

He asked Him to bless me, protect me,

save my soul, keep me within the wings of Him,

never leave nor forsake me and continue to love me

My man, my love, this intriguing

genuinely lovely man

Exposed his heart, his vulnerabilities, his nakedness

before our Mighty God

This man

now speaking in a love language

I know not of

Pouring all of himself out for me

Covering me, loving me Agape,

being one with Holy Spirt and Christ for me

I begin reeling from the sensation of how much this man

this particular man

my spouse, my head my covering

This man

Who places my spiritual wellbeing before his own

This man

Who is not afraid to allow me to know that

he prays for me

Fights battles for me

stands in the gap for me

I have never known a man could love like this

The love of a man for his woman

No

the love of a husband for his wife

This is so new, fresh, strong, sensual, pleasing

generous, and giving

My tears could not be staunched

Nothing held the flood gates closed

The power of him moved me…

My man ends his prayer in that special language

I hear him stir and he opens the door

I glance up at his face and through the blinds in my room

the moon casts a delicate golden glow upon him

Was this the moon

or the power of the throne room

in the presence of God!

I espied the tears pouring forth from him

He could not quench the flow

His body quivering, his head bowed low

A moment passed and he lifted his head

He was different

His countenance held one of wonder

I began to feel the presence of the Holy Spirit

as my tears continued

I arose from the bed and stood before this man

This glorious man, who was touched by God

This glorious man who humbled himself

and lay at the alter

Wow,

I did not understand the wonder of his experience

I could only see the after

He grabbed my hand and

Tenderly

kissed it

He drew me closer as the tears continued

Neither of us able

to contain it

bound by the presence of God

Neither of us willing to breathe or speak

We, the two of us becoming one in Spirit

The two of us **BECOMING**

It seemed as if time stood still

that we were no longer present within this realm

Finally, he took a deep breath

I continued my gaze upon him

He looked at me with the stains of fresh tears

eyes red

and spoke these words…

"I LOVE YOU AS CHRIST SO LOVED THE CHURCH."

Patricia Johnson

Hallelujah, Praise God

I found myself in a space unknown to me

filled with sounds

movement

people speaking

but I could not understand

my hands I could not move

my voice could not be heard

what's going on

I don't understand

I was awake

Lord God, help me

I reached out my hand

but I'm secured by the straps

all I could do was reach my fingers toward heaven

as I made my plea

I hear these people in white

they tell my man

nothing more they can do

His eyes rest on my face

Can't he see

I am here

I can hear what is being said

I am alive, I am breathing

Her Name is Grace

I am here

My husband continued to peruse my face

he moved closer to me

He reached a hand and slid it across my brow

bent closer to kiss my lips

He leaned into me and pressed his face against my ear

Don't give up

Fight

Fight for me

Fight for our children

I need you; you are the better half of me

I desire to have you my love

whole and free

You are my woman, my wife

my good thing

Don't give up, keep fighting

I know God may be calling you home,

but I need you

I need you here with me

ask him to allow you more time

I know that's selfish of me

I love you

His tears began to fall upon my face

I could feel the pain and agony in him

and tried to speak

I tried to dispel his fears

But I could not move

the voice was not heard, but I could hear, see, and feel

My spirit was alive, my body weak

I am here

Please fight for me

Pray for me

Can't you hear me

As those thoughts rose in my heart

my husband fell to his knees

bowed his head and cried out for me

My voice was heard.

Nothing gets by our God.

My husband began pleading on my behalf

God heard his supplications to spare his wife

the love of his life

God heard his tears and felt his pain

God heard, felt, and understood this man's love for his wife

for me

My man could not take it

He looked up at me with so much love

not understanding

I could see, and hear but could not speak

My man, my Black man, roared upon his knees

Singing out praises to our God

Our Healer

Hallelujah became his continued praise

He replaced his pleas with praise of gratitude

for my healing

Flowing in faith

He continued to praise God amid the storm

When it seemed like all hope was gone

He did not give up or give in

he was taken with the wind

His praise raised to another level

a new dimension

The power of his praise and the ferocity he displayed

caused the room to shake

the windows shattered

and the bonds that held me

released

His praise was so intense he never heard the alarms go off

and the nurses run in

They tried to stop his praise, but his worship was fierce glorifying God he could not resist

As his praise continued

I was freed

My voice, though raspy

my throat raw

I managed to whisper the words

"HALLELUJAH, PRAISE GOD!"

Special Acknowledgment

Tiffany,

You are more than an editor, writer, family, friend, or sister in Christ. You are a gift from God that happens to be in love with what you do. Your wisdom, knowledge and dedication to God's excellence helped to uncover parts of me that I could not see. Your blessing and humility always draw me closer to you. Your gift is so natural, and I was not afraid or overly concerned with your suggestions because it helped me to make God's work, not Patricia's, excellent. You caused me to see how one word or rearranging a phrase gives more potency to what I am trying to express.

Your sincere desire to help me unlock what God placed in me taught me so much about grammar and editing but more about the power and dimension that words can take you. You are someone that is highly favored at your craft, and it is my hope that God continues to blow your mind with where He is taking you.

You helped me, as a midwife, to clean my baby after its birth and to prepare her to be presented, first back to God then to the world.

I give all the honor and glory to God for allowing us to collaborate and bring to pass a work of excellence that will change the life of many.

Again, my heartfelt thanks and I love you!

About the Author

Patricia Johnson is a native of Baltimore. She is an Author, Activist, Motivational Speaker, Columnist, and volunteer at the National Alliance on Mental Illness (NAMI). She is also a member of the Phi Theta Kappa Honor Society, CCBC Alumni Association, and Women in Philanthropy. In addition, she has received her Behavioral Health Counseling Advanced Certificate and a Human Services Generalist Certificate.

She desires to expose the impact of domestic violence upon her battered body and her state of mind. Patricia had Personality Disorder, Depression, and Post Traumatic Stress Disorder, which led to a suicide attempt.

Domestic violence violates women, young and old. The spectrum is broad, and demographics have no boundaries. Socioeconomic status, culture, ethnicity, and religion are irrelevant. It is breathing, living, and exudes power and wishes to consume anyone in its path.

She hopes that through her life story, eyes will open to the plight of our teenage victims. Patricia believes that if we can heal our daughters, there will be fewer battered women in the future.

Her first book, "Broken and Battered Yet I Rise," consists of stories of her life in a poetic format that narrates her state of mind and experiences as a battered wife. You will feel her pain as she maneuvered through life's perils at home, church, work, and prison, as well as her victory. Finally, God removed a half-million-dollar mountain to grant her freedom. Journey with her as she soars from the depths of pain and sorrow through the doors of the Maryland Department of Corrections for Women STRENGTHENED, EMPOWERED, RENEWED, VALUED, and ENCOURAGED. She rises still, fortified by the knowledge of who she was in Christ Jesus and a child of God.

Patricia is also an avid writer of other types of Christian stories; she has just released "The Marriage Bed Undefiled, My Sensual Self, Through Poetic Freedom." Again, God has given her something so amazing, precious, and unique. It's one thing to teach or tell a story through writing; it's another to make learning beautiful; He has given Patricia the ability to do just that.

It is by, through, and because of the mighty hand of our Lord and Savior Jesus Christ that she can expose her journey within the folds of her books.

Also By the Author

Broken and Battered Yet I Rise: A Synopsis Through Poetry in
the Life of a Battered Wife

(Is God in the Home of a Battered Wife - Book 2)

The Marriage Bed Undefiled: My Sensual Self Through Poetic
Freedom

Sister2Sister: How I Became a 5th Commandment Child